Theodore Nickline Eaton

The Good Shepherd

A Church Service in Song, and Other Verses

-

Theodore Nickline Eaton

The Good Shepherd
A Church Service in Song, and Other Verses

ISBN/EAN: 9783744799362

Printed in Europe, USA, Canada, Australia, Japan

Cover: Foto ©Thomas Meinert / pixelio.de

More available books at **www.hansebooks.com**

Yours Truly
Sheldon N. Eaton

THE GOOD SHEPHERD,

A CHURCH SERVICE IN SONG,

AND

OTHER VERSES.

BY

THEODORE N. EATON,

PASTOR FIRST METHODIST EPISCOPAL CHURCH,

McKEESPORT, PA.

1899

1899:
DAILY NEWS PUBLISHING COMPANY,
MCKEESPORT PA.

CONTENTS.

THE GOOD SHEPHERD,

A CHURCH SERVICE IN SONG.

Opening Hymn.

INTO thy courts, O God, we come
    With reverential fear,
That we may bring an offering
And unto thee draw near.

In vain we offer prayer and praise
    If thou dost not inspire,
If on the altar of our hearts
    Thou dost not kindle fire.

Behold, O God, the altar now,
    Let fire from heaven descend,
While in thy house, as worshipers,
    Repentant sinners bend.

O let it be the glorious sign
    Of thy forgiving love,
That drives out all impurity
    And lifts the heart above.

Prayer.

ALMIGHTY and everlasting God, who, of thy tender love towards mankind, hast sent thy Son, our Savior Jesus Christ, to take upon him our flesh, and to suffer death upon the cross, that all mankind should follow the example of his great humility; mercifully grant, that we may both follow the example of his patience, and also be made partakers of his resurrection; through Jesus Christ Our Lord. *Amen.*

Almighty God, who hast given thine only Son to be unto us both a sacrifice for sin, and an example of Godly life; give us grace that we may always most thankfully receive that his inestimable benefit, and also daily endeavor to follow the blessed steps of his most holy life; through Jesus Christ our Lord. *Amen.*

Our Father who art in heaven, hallowed be thy name. Thy kingdom come. Thy will be done in earth, as it is in heaven. Give us this day our daily bread; and forgive us our trespasses, as we forgive them that trespass against us; and lead us not into temptation, but deliver us from evil; for thine is the kingdom, and the power, and the glory forever. *Amen.*

Psalm.

THE Lord is my shepherd; I shall not want.
He maketh me to lie down in green pastures:
he leadeth me beside the still waters.

He restoreth me my soul: he leadeth me in the paths of righteousness for his name's sake.

Yea, though I walk through the valley of the shadow of death, I will fear no evil: for thou art with me; thy rod and thy staff they comfort me.

Thou preparest a table before me in the presence of mine enemies: thou anointest my head with oil; my cup runneth over.

Surely goodness and mercy shall follow me all the days of my life: and I will dwell in the house of the Lord forever.

—Psalms XXIII.

Gloria Patri.

GLORY be to the Father, and to the Son, and to the Holy Ghost; as it was in the beginning, is now, and ever shall be, world without end.   Amen.

Gospel.

VERILY, verily, I say unto you, He that entereth not by the door into the sheepfold, but climbeth up some other way, the same is a thief and a robber.

But he that entereth in by the door is the shepherd of the sheep.

To him the porter openeth; and the sheep hear his voice: and he calleth his own sheep by name, and leadeth them out.

And when he putteth forth his own sheep, he goeth before them, and the sheep follow him: for they know his voice.

And a stranger will they not follow, but will flee from him; for they know not the voice of strangers.

I am the good shepherd, and know my sheep, and am known of mine.

As the Father knoweth me, even so know I the Father: and I lay down my life for the sheep.

And other sheep I have, which are not of this fold: them also must I bring, and they shall hear my voice; and there shall be one fold, and one shepherd.

—St. John X: 1-5, 14-16.

Anthem.

God of our fathers, thee we praise,
  Into thy gracious presence come;
To thee great King, our hearts we raise,
  As low we bend before thy throne:
  O Lord, our God, thy Blessings send,
  As low we bend, as low we bend.

Though human voices ne'er can sing
  Such strains as set thy glory forth,
Nor prayers that men can ever bring
  Declare the splendor of thy reign,
    O Lord, our God, thy blessings send,
    As low we bend, as low we bend.

No other incense can we burn,   .
  Nor offering on thine altars lay,
Than hearts disposed from sin to turn
  And trust in our redeeming Lord:
    O Lord, our God, thy blessings send,
    As low we bend, as low we be bend.

Thou dost invite; thy spirit cries,
  "Let all the heavy-laden come!

Who on my word, my love relies
   Shall never from my face be driven:"
     O Lord, our God, thy blessings send,
     As low we bend, as low we bend.

O let us ne'er forget thy love,
   Nor yet thy gracious counsel shun;
Send us thy Spirit from above,
   And fix in us thine own abode,
     That we may Abba, Father cry,
     And ever on thy strength rely.   Amen.

---

*Adapted to DeKoven's Recessional music.

Text.

And when he putteth forth his own sheep, he goeth before them, and the sheep follow him, for they know his voice. JOHN x:4.

Sermon.

THE orient shepherds built, with prudent care,
  Their ample folds, well walled around, that there,
  .Not distant from abodes of men, each night,
From evening's hush till morning's mellow light,
With doors made fast, their flocks of gentle sheep
And tender lambs, secure, in peace might sleep.

His station at the door, or on the walls,
As faithful as the watch in princely halls,
A porter, who, with ear attent, would hear
And bravely guard, if any foe came near.

Here, gathered from the distant plain and hill,
From pastures green and from the waters still,
As night drew near, the gentle flocks, well fed,
And each one by its faithful shepherd led,
Were brought within the fold, that all might rest

Together as one flock, and then in quest,
Of frugal evening meal, each watcher sought
His humble peasant home and, with no thought
Of care, hunger appeased, at his behest
There came the angel Sleep to bring him rest.

When now the western firmament, that shone
With gold and crimson glories all her own,
Has lost the splendor of her evening hues,
And perfumed skies distilled and dropped their dews
Upon a slumbering earth; when stars have kept
Their all-night vigils over men who slept;
Ere yet the sun his fiery form has pressed
Above earth's far off eastern edge and blessed
The world with fulness of another day;
Before the mellow twilight spreads its grey
In such profusion as to light the way;
The shepherd, waking from his dreamless stay
In peaceful slumber-land, once more is roused
To thought of those which yester' e'en he housed
Within the friendly shelter of the fold.

Because he loves the sheep, and not for gold,
His eyes no more to slumber bands he yields;
Intent to lead his flock to pasture fields,

From simple store of food his fast he breaks,
And hastens to the fold ere day awakes.

To him the porter opens wide the door;
He enters and with call oft heard before,
Not long, nor loud, but wonderfully sweet,
He stirs the slumbering flocks a friend to greet.
To some his voice no welcome accent brings;
They know him not, nor know the notes he sings;
But ears there are which hear as if some strain
Of well known melody were sung again;
When called by name with eager haste they run—
For so the shepherd designates each one—
And follow him, whatever way he wends,
As men would follow tried and trusted friends.

He journeys with them toward the mountain side,
Where grows the grass in meadows green and wide:
But far away those pasture lands are found,
And many a rough, steep, pathway, winding round
In tortuous and uncertain course, they tread:
About them, dense and dark, the forests spread:
Because the mountain is with rocks begirt,
Full many a precipice they closely skirt;

They clamber over rocks o'ergrown with moss,
And dashing mountain streams they leap across
Before they reach the journey's end, and stand
In safety in the mountain meadow land.

His Cross.

Our Lord, who knew
Of shepherds true,
Who led their sheep,
By pathways steep,
To pastures wide,
On mountain side,
Hath said, that, "When he putteth forth his own,
The sheep that hear his voice and know his call,
He sends them not to try the way alone,
But goes before and knows and cares for all."
Thus may we know,
Who onward go,
O'er life's rough roads,
With heavy loads;
Whate'er the way
We walk today,
Our feet shall not
Press any spot,
By Him untried;
Unsanctified
By footprints of
Him whom we love.

A WEARY wanderer through the fields of time,
I grope my way amid a dark world's grime;
In dangerous and toilsome paths I tread,
Life filled with burden, soul oppressed with dread,
Until, sometimes, I almost ask release,
Release from burden and from fear surcease;
Then pause and try God's purposes to scan,
And feel, that once to understand his plan,
To know why in such ways my lot should fall,
'Twere easier, with brave heart, to meet it all;
To face the thousand ills which mar my life,
And calm and peaceful front all mundane strife.

  Why might I not begin my life to train
In some fair world entirely free from stain?
Why should I ever stand with danger girt?
Why wearily contend with foes alert?
Why must I, in a straight and narrow path,
With solemn dread of everlasting wrath,
My wayward life, with constant effort, press—
As many things to burden as to bless—
While, everywhere, broad paths of danger lie,
With beauty fringed, to tempt me from the sky?

Nor am I first in undertaking quest
For answer, which might bring the troubled rest;
Before the priestly office and the church,
As old as heartache, older still the search;
As old as sin, distrust, despair and grief,
When sacred promise brought but slight relief,
These questions are. The thoughtful of all time,
The tempted, troubled, tried, of every clime,
Have asked, with throbbing heart and anxious mind,
Why God should choose for helpless human kind
A world with evil filled as training place;
Why doom to pain and death a human race.

In all the passing years, no answer came;
Philosopher and sage could nothing frame
Of helpful words with power to bring content
To struggling ones, however well was meant
Their idle work of spinning theories,
Which make us see but men as walking trees;
And those, who, in their agony, have cried
To heaven as humble suppliants, have died
Before a message came to solve their doubt,
Drive gloom away, and put their fear to rout.

Down deep in nature's heart the causes lie:

We cannot fathom though with tears we try
Her depths; but left to comfort us is trust
That God, the God of nature, still is just;
And, when, with earnest gaze, we search the sea
Of our own inner life, there can but be
Reflected back such picture as will tell
To all, who know to read the spirit well,
That God, who sends all worlds to whirl in space,
Who fixes fast their bounds, decrees their pace,
And makes them sing, in glorious strain, his praise,
In anthems such as morning stars can raise,
And settles all their destiny forever,
Though He be infinite in power, can never
To kinship with himself our spirits bring,
Or make it possible due praise to sing,
Until—our moral worth securely fixed
By choices free, where strangely mixed
The good and evil intertwined lie—
Our spirits dare to claim such kinship high.

    We walk by faith; we cannot walk by sight;
Here will I rest, in darkness of this night,
Though not a single star can send its ray
Through cloudy skies, which overhang the way:
The soul of things is good, and God above,

Who made this world and fashioned us, is love.
He plans no evil thing, and this world's strife
Must, somehow, issue in a better life.

It shall not give me fret that mountain peaks
Show broader, grander, views to him who seeks
Their summits, than the level plain can give
To men content forever there to live;
Nor shall my soul be vexed that meadows lie,
Sometimes, on mountain slopes, while, parched and dry,
The plain below, unfruitful fields and bare,
Spreads out, where none may feed; nor shall I dare
Give place to plaint because within the wall,
Secure and strong, there is not food for all
The flocks which, mingling, rest in safety there,
Protected by a faithful porter's care.

I try no more the mystery to solve;
Within my mind no more dark thoughts revolve,
Because I know the shepherd-spirit, kind,
Has put me forth in these rough ways to find
The pastures green; and I, with strength conceived
And born of hope, as one who has believed
The.glad report that all is done in love,
With eyes forever fixed on things above,

Will gladly toil; will every danger face;
And run with patient joy the weary race,
Because into the life the blessed know
No man without these things could ever grow;
For this the Shepherd puts me forth to try
The dangers and the toil of mountains high.

What seems but ill,
    In all our storm and stress,
    Comes after all to bless:
My soul be still.

The heart's best thrill
    Of joy is felt, at last,
    When pain endured is past:
Trust and be still.

It is God's will
    That stress, and storm, and pain,
    Should never come in vain:
Trust and be still.

Trust and be still;
    And let pain, stress and storm
    Give thee each day the form
That suits his will.

A S when the shepherd putteth forth his own,
And bids them walk in ways before unknown,
He goes before them, and they hear his voice
And follow him, so, I in this rejoice;
The Lord, our Shepherd, in the heavy lore
Of sorrow deeply learned is.   The core
Of earth's most bitter fruit is to his taste
Familiar, and the trials which lay waste
Our lives were burdens which he bravely bore:
In all these ways, our shepherd goes before.
We do not journey any road untried
By him.   A foe whom he has not defied
We shall not meet.   Whatever ills we bear
Have darkened old Judea's roadway where
The Master entered it and walked along.
We sing no minor strain of saddened song,
We strike no note of sorrow, that would not
Find melancholy chord in all his lot.
'Tis this of which the sacred penman writes,
When he for us the sacred words indites:
"For it became him for whom all things are,
In bringing many sons from earth afar,
Him by whom all things have their being here,

In bringing sons to glory, who are dear
To him, to make the Captain of the host,
Him in whose life and love and death they boast,
A perfect Prophet, Priest and King,
A perfect Savior, through his suffering."

Cease thy lament, O, child of earth.
Compare thy lot with his, who had his birth
In Bethlehem; who taught in Gallilee,
Jerusalem, and on the stormy sea
Genesaret; and, in Judea, wrought,
In love, the wondrous cure of all who sought
His sovereign power in healing arts,
And spoke his word of peace to troubled hearts.

Dost thou know what it is for bread to toil,
And, art thou sick at heart of this world's moil?
The Master's hand has pushed the plane,
And held the hammer and the nails, and stain
Of labor been upon his coarse, cheap dress,
While he, with humble, loyal faithfulness
To Joseph, took the place of first born son,
And found in work disgrace, or burden, none.

Hast thou for home a very humble place?
Has fortune failed thee?   In the wild, mad race

For earthly gain hast fallen far behind?
Thou still hast riches more, in every kind
Of present treasure, than our Lord, who said:
"The Son of man hath not whereon his head
May lie, while e'en the birds have nests,
And the wild fox the hole wherein he rests."
At Bethany and in Capernaum
Love opened humble doors that he might come
Within, an honored friend, and, there, find rest
Among the lowly ones, who loved him best;
Or, there, awhile, precarious shelter take
From growing plots, which envious priests did make
Against him and his messianic throne;
But often he would spend the night alone
Upon some quite deserted mountain side;
Or, with the men he loved, at eventide,
Would wend his way across the Kedron vale,
Into the garden, where was heard his wail
Of bitter struggle with the powers of night,
And, sheltered by the trees, would wait the light.

Oh, Garden of the Olive Press,
Gethsemane, on Olivet,
Thy trees still stand but ne'er confess,

To waiting souls their words might bless,
    The things they know so well.

There, underneath thy spreading shade,
    Sweet, sad Gethsemane,
Upon thy sod, my Master laid
His weary form, or all night prayed,
    As was his wont, to God.

What things he said, what joy he knew—
    Sweet, glad Gethsemane—
What rest he found, what comfort true,
Might seem to us forever new,
    If thou couldst tell us all.

    O Son of God, thou Son of man, who world
On world, with God-like skill and power, hast hurled
Out into space, in regions far beyond
The sight of men, and fastened, with the bond
Of thine own word, the stars to shine above,
Abjectly poor didst thou become, in love
For us, that, through thy want and woe, all we,
Who love and trust thee in thy poverty,
Made rich, might see the wonders of thy grace
As manifested to a ruined race.

Hast thou in life known burden hard to bear?
Which of thy burdens now shall we compare
With the tremendous loads which Jesus bore,
Until, at last, the heart, which long was sore,
No longer able to endure its grief,
Did break, and thus in death he found relief.

Has every fiber of thy soul been rent
By trials and temptations Satan-sent?
E'en yet thou hast not suffered more
In all thy years than Jesus did of yore,
When, in the forty days of varied test,
Satan besought him yield to his behest;
Or, in Gethsemane, sore pressed, he prayed,
And like a devastating wave, unstayed
By rugged ocean shores, o'er him there came
The agony that swept and swayed his frame.

O, Garden of the Agony,
Gethsemane, on Olivet,
Such story thou couldst tell to me
Of anguish, as should make me see
What things my Lord endured.

There, underneath thy spreading trees,
Sad, sad Gethsemane,

He drank the cup down to the lees,
The cup of bitterness, beneath thy trees,
And said, "Thy will be done."

Hast thou been undervalued and unsought,
Maligned, insulted, spit upon, and brought
Into disgrace?   Have brethren foes become,
Friends spoken slightingly, left thee alone?
Hast thou been buffeted with cruel hand?
As crown upon thy brow, a twisted band
Of thorns pressed down, until great drops of red
From currents of thine own life stained thy head;
And on thy shoulder has the cross been borne
Till, by the wayside, fainting and forlorn,
Thou stumbledst and fell down; and, hast thou known
The awful hour, when God left thee alone;
When from thy lips was forced the plaintive cry,
"My God, why hast thou left me thus, alone, to try
My strength 'gainst those whose highest joy is strife,
Unaided by thy presence, which is life?"
In all, thou hast not suffered more than he,
Who bore thy sins upon the accursed tree.

But we could better bear the ills, which throng
Our way in life, than meet the Giant, strong,

Defiant, proud, of fearful mien, whose glance
Hath power to wither all. Men name him Death,
And speak the name with awe and bated breath.
His dwelling place the grave, dark, loathsome, dread;
Its cavern floors with skeletons are spread.
He daily sallies forth and thousands fall;
His presence doth the stoutest heart appall.
Thanks be to God, who ne'er deserts his own,
We need not meet this enemy alone:
The Master, to the tomb, as everywhere,
Has gone before us, and, in conflict there,
Has overcome: there, in its fearful shade,
Has waged a warfare which has laid
The Giant, Death, prostrate, defeated, low;
At touch divine, a fully conquered foe.

Look thou, O, man—thou who dost stand in dread,
Lest he, who bears the glass and scythe, with tread
Relentless come thy way, and cut thy stalk
Of unripe life, and o'er it rudely walk,
And none be found to run to thy relief;
This man of sorrows and acquaint with grief
Has walked the weary way of life throughout:
Now, at the end, in triumph hear him shout,
"O, Grave! where is thy victory; and where,

O, Death, thy sting?"   From open sepulcher
He cries to us, "Henceforth the tomb, I leave,
Is not a prison-house, nor shall men weave
About it dreadful thoughts;" and all the place
He fills with glorious light, while, by his grace,
We write above its door, these words of cheer,
"Fear not ye mortals when ye enter here."

Our Cross.

Thus was it written,
To calm the smitten;
Bitter to sweeten;
Dark days to brighten;
Burdens to lighten;—
"The shepherd when he putteth forth his own,
The sheep that hear his voice, to him are known,
Goes on before." He sends them not alone,
And thus we know,
Our feet shall go,
In no rough way,
In our own day,
That was not trod,
O, Son of God,
By thee, alone,
When to atone
For guilty man,
And lift the ban,
Thou walked this way
In thine own day.

THE shepherd goes, not far away, before,
  And lingers, waiting until all cross o'er
  The streams.   The bleating of the weary lamb
He hears, and quickly gathers it to calm
And safe repose within a generous fold
Of his own mantle.   Weary ones, and old,
He makes the object of his special care.
He journeys slowly up the hills and where
The way is steep or rough; and, if a sheep,
By wandering far, be lost, he will not sleep,
But leave the ninety and the nine, to rest
Within the fold, and go, in patient quest,
To seek the one, on lonely mountain side,
And when he finds the wand'rer, far and wide
His joyous song resounds, and friends rejoice
When echoes back to them the shepherd's voice.

  So may we feel assured that, in our hours
Of greatest need, our Shepherd's care is ours.
He goes not far before; he hears our cry;
Ready to meet our want is ever nigh.

  When has the Master been so near to thee,
As when it was so dark thou couldst not see

To find thy way along life's path, and, in
Thy troubled dream, didst cry aloud to him,
"O, Master, help! or, I, thy child, am lost."

He nearest is to those who, tempest tossed,
Most feel the need of help; to those who bear
The heavy burden most; to those who wear
The mourner's weeds, and those who are contrite.
The heart of man doth not grow mellow quite
Till God sends sorrow as the ripening frost;
The highest things are purchased at such cost.

If challenged to the proof that thus our Lord
Is near to those who walk in sweet accord
With him, in hours of peril and distress,
When fortune fails and enemies oppress,
The story of ten thousand martyr lives,
Writ long ago in sanguinary lines,
Illuminated by divinest light,
Beyond a possible defeasance might
Establish all our claim.   The prototype
Of all the holy martyr race, first ripe
Of all for Heaven, the victim of the hate
Of those who vengeance breathed and were irate
Against our Lord and all who honored him,

Held him not nearer, when, in distance dim,
The parted clouds and riven vault of blue
Yielded his steadfast gaze their vision true,
Than multitudes, in after years, who thought
Not life itself so dear it should be bought
At cost of cursing him who brought to light
That life which ends no more in death's dread night.

   Could we, who, spirits willing, yet to earth
Are fastened by our bodies from our birth
Until released by death—could we, made light
As angels are and giv'n angelic sight,
But soar o'er earth to scan its history,
Observing all, as angels do; then would we see,
In every chamber where the sick abide;
By every mother at a cradle side
When death comes near; in every busy mart
Where noble men have seen their wealth depart;
In each unequal struggle where the good
Have met misfortune; one has stood—
Unseen by vulgar eyes, hid from the gaze
Of careless ones, with form of radiant grace
And beauty, crowned and clothed in light of heaven—
Stood to fulfill the ancient promise given—
Given to his own before he did ascend

To heaven, "Lo, I am with you to the end!"
Then should we know that, in all burdened years,
No man, with honest soul and bitter tears,
Has tried to hold the current of his life,
With firm hand, steady, where the fearful strife
Is made unequal by the might of foes;
Nor any soul, enduring trial throes,
Stood firm, despite his nature's wayward trend,
Against the wiles of Satan, who would bend
Our lives, red-heated in the furnace of
Temptation, to the ugly form and love
Of things which would destroy; nor any man
Of upward look and high and holy plan,
Between the nether millstone of desire
And upper stone of what God's laws require
Been ground; but that the eye of faith could see,
Quite near, that radiant presence—it was he
Who, in the furnace sevenfold hot, was seen
As fourth; whose presence was the fireproof screen
Which saved the holy Hebrew three, when swathed
In flames, and brought them off unscathed;
Nor has a Christian come to death's dark vale,
But it was turned by Him into a dale,
Cool, shadowy and peaceful, and the Son of God
Made the way easy by his staff and rod.

Shall we complain because we tread rough ways,
In climbing to the mountain top and blaze
Of splendor, which shall there surround and light,
With glory all ineffable and bright,
Our joyous lives, redeemed forever more?
Nay, but rejoice, because "He goes before."

Closing Hymn.

WITH joy we entered, Lord, thy house,
That we might worship there;
In peace, now bid us all depart,
Under thy watchful care.

If thou shalt lead to pastures green,
Or by the waters still,
Help us, with thankful hearts, to go
Obedient to thy will.

But if thou lead by pathways rough,
O, may we nothing fear,
But trust the promise thou hast given,
Forever to be near.

In peace now bid us all depart,
As here with joy we came:
Teach us to rest in thy great love,
Forever more the same.

Benediction.

Now the God of peace that brought again from the dead Our Lord Jesus, that great Shepherd of the sheep, through the blood of the everlasting covenant, make you perfect in every good work to do his will, working in you that which is well pleasing in his sight; through Jesus Christ, to whom be glory for ever and ever.   Amen.

OTHER VERSES.

Finding the Christ-Child.

I

I heard the story of the Christ-child's birth,
  And prayed, "Kind Shepherds, O show me
  Where babe and Madonna may be,
For they say that the Christ-child came to earth,

    Came to speak to me."
    A sad voice replied,
    "The shepherds have died,
  And do not hear thee."

II

Much grieved that shepherds could not hear my prayer,
  I cried, "O Wise Men, happy band,
  Who, coming from a far-off land,
The Christ-child found, O, show me where

    Is the sacred spot."
    Again the voice said,
    "The Wise Men are dead,
  And they hear thee not."

III

Heart sick because no help could come from men;
  "Angels, who sang the Christ-child's birth,
  Come back once more, come back to earth,"
I cried, "Sing me your song of peace again,

    And show me the way."
      Once more the voice spoke,
      "Why angels invoke?
    They come not today."

IV

My heart no more from breaking could I keep:
  I sat down beside another,
  One who sought and found not, brother
To him in his grief, and turned aside to weep:

    I heard a low sound;
      A voice sweet and mild,
      "I am the Christ-child,"
    It said, "thou hast found."

III

Doubt and Good Cheer.

THE funeral dirge of faith
   Sadly sang a maiden,
'Mid the wrack and wraith
   Of her early Aiden,
     In the autumn:—

"Away from their empty, dangling nests,
   The birds are flown into fathomless air
As out of its old belief and rest
   My soul has wandered—where?"

A song of abiding cheer,
   Though the leaves were falling,
Sang one who sat near,
   But heard glad voices calling
     From the springtime:—

'Again to rebuild their dangling nests
   Shall the birds come back in the springtime fair;
So the soul, that once by faith was blest,
   Never, forever, shall despair.'

Storm and Sunshine.

A S rain and sunshine, wind and storm
   All shape the growing tree,
And make its trunk and spreading form
   The generous thing we see,

Under whose shade the weary rest
   When fainting by the way;
So storm and sunshine should give zest
   To growing men, who may,

In after years, when stress has brought
   To them that splendid form,
Which never can by ease be wrought,
   But grows alone in storm,

Be like the tree which stands to say,
   To every weary one,
"Beneath my branches here you may
   Be sheltered from the sun."

Like a Vapor.

L IKE a morning vapor rising from the stream,
         Misty, vague, uncertain;
         Fleecy, silken curtain,
Hanging for a moment, fading like a dream,
         Is the life of man.

But the breath of heaven, in earth's valleys chilled,
         Winter-bound and lonely,
         Here appearing only
Till the morning warms it, as our God hath willed;
         Such the life of man.

See, the mist can tarry but a little time:
         Silent, stealthy, certain,
         Lifts the fleecy curtain;
In a moment pass we to another clime;
         Pass the sons of men.
Say not thou tomorrow; morrow may not dawn;
         Let today be brightened
         By a life well rightened,
For if comes tomorrow, you may then be gone—
         Gone beyond earth's ken.

The Old Preacher.

AS the years crept on with a sure, steady pace,
   The preacher, who had been a giant in strength,
   Had stooped, become grey, and grown pallid of face,
   Until he had fallen, and lay there at length,
Prone on his couch, like some hero whose power
Had vanished, and left him robbed of his dower.

   In time long gone by, with his heart stirred by love,
   He felt himself called, as a herald of truth,
   To bear news of salvation from heaven above;
   Had given unstinted both manhood and youth;
Now old he lies dying; soon all will be o'er,
And he will have crossed to the other shore.

   He lingers, and dreams of some scene in the past;
   Of people assembled, and church lacking light;
   Of himself as reluctant, but compelled at the last;
   And murmurs: *"There will be no preaching tonight."
Ah! Tonight there will be no preaching 'tis true,
But heaven will dawn on the old preacher's view.

---

*The last words of the Rev. Dr. D. L. Dempsey.

The lights are gone out, the doors are shut close,
    The key has been turned in the rusty old lock;
The preacher, gone forth to the grave, finds repose;
    New voices must plead, others point to the Rock
On which men shall stand, to the One who gives light;
By him there will no more be preaching tonight.

The Last Word.*

LET it be recorded, shine forth as the light,
    Where'er sin has shrouded mortal man in night,
Jesus is a refuge, thither men may flee;
    He can loose their fetters, he can set them free.

Let it be recorded, graven in the stone,
    Where'er hearts are aching, where is heard a moan,
Jesus Christ can comfort all who are in tears;
    He can bear their sorrows, he can calm their fears.

Let it be recorded, where'er doubt is rife,
    Where'er men are longing for immortal life;
Tell them Christ has conquered, cast down death and hell—
    Tell them they may join him angel ranks to swell.

Let it be recorded, graven well in stone,
    Shout aloud the message, "Jesus died to atone:"
Preach, and sing, and tell he triumphed o'er the grave;
    Nowhere is a sinner, Jesus cannot save.

---

*The venerable Dr. Samuel Wakfield, who died in his ninety-sixth year, said, as his last coherent utterance, "I want to put it on record that there is no sinner so low but Jesus can save him."

Our Hope.

WE live in a world by shadows o'er cast;
  Where night follows day with all too great haste;
Where winter chills summer with ruthless blast,
  And makes of all nature wide spreading waste;

Where childhood vanishes like morning dew;
  Where youth with its buoyancy soon fades away;
While manhood bears burdens that ever are new,
  And age with its weariness closes life's day;

Where death follows fast and in frigid embrace
  Each mortal holds hard to his chilly breast;
And thus hurries on each man of the race
  To find in the grave his earliest rest:

But the hope of the Christian mounts up to the skies,
  To a home where there comes neither winter nor night;
Where no one grows old, and no one e'er dies,
  And all is enduring, immortal and bright.

My Heart Crieth Out.

THE gates of life swung open wide,
  One day, upon a new made land;
  A living soul came in; and then, to hide
From mortal eyes, by God's command,
The regions back of life, the over-world,
  The angel standing there to guard,
To duty's call responsive, quickly hurled
  Them shut again, and then stood ward.

The brazen gates of death swung open soon
  To let that soul slip out again,
When—by divine command, to keep the boon
  Of knowledge from the sons of men,
To hide from sight the borders of the land
  Where spirits dwell—the somber guard,
An angel who stands there with eager hand,
  Quick shut the gate, and then stood ward.

And with a faithfulness divinely true,
  Those wards have stood and guarded so
The gates of life and death, the ages through,

That when men come, and when men go,
No careless moment do they stand ajar
   To show us either start or goal,
The mystic regions, shimmering lands afar,
   The whence and whither of the soul.

But long ago there dawned a day so bright,
   That one, who looked with eager care
Into himself, and learned to read aright,
   What had been always written there,
Could see, deep-chisled on the walls
   Of inmost rooms, indellibly,
What, whosoever treads these inner halls,
   Must read,—GOD,—IMMORTALITY.

Sabbath Evening Hymn.

MY soul, awake and sing:
Bring praises to our King
With gladsome sound:
His mercy and his grace,
Extended to our race,
With rolling years keep pace,
To us abound.

Another day of days,
A Sabbath filled with praise,
E'en now is past:
In home and temple fair,
Have mingled hymn and prayer,
While we, with joy, our care
On Him have cast.

As shadows gather 'round,
May love and peace abound
In every heart;
God give us sleep tonight;

Keep us till morning light;
And never from the right
    Let us depart.

When Sabbath days are o'er,
And we on earth no more
    May meet to pray;
In richer, happier lays,
With angels may we raise,
In heaven, our song of praise,
    Through endless days.

DOXOLOGY.

We praise thee, Father, Son,
And Spirit, Three in One,
    And thee alone;
While all before thee bend,
To us thy presence lend,
And let our song ascend
    Up to thy throne.

God's Acre.

"GOD's acre" they call the field
    Where the bodies of men, asleep,
    Now lie waiting till earth shall yield
Her precious stores, and even the Deep —
    Old Ocean—shall give up the dead
    Who lie on hidden sea mosses,
    Resting as sleepers in bed
When night hours are dreamlessly peaceful.

    What ground shall bring forth
    Fruit of such worth,
    When trumpeter's call
    The harvesters all,
To glean, in God's fields, for heaven's great store
Of spirits immortal and blest evermore,
    As "God's acre?"

"God's acre" has grown until,
    By thousands, now, we number
The broad acres of valley, hill,
    And well shaded slope, where slumber

Somebody's dear friends and loved ones,
With no one sleeping so soundly
But all shall hear the summons
To rise and meet the king, in mid-air.

In these broad acres shall these reapers,
From seed thus sown,
All gather God's own,
And there shall be garnered a store of sheaves,
In number far greater than rich autumn's leaves,
From God's thousand acres.

III

To An Old Violin.

COME tell me—speak slowly and lowly, in whispers, old fiddle—
The secret thou holdest so long, come tell me thy riddle.

Neck slender and shapely, thy amber shining and golden,
Bouts well proportioned, delicate purfling, workmanship olden,

Thou seemest but beech, spruce, and eb'ny, a thing of mere wood
Deftly united, with gut strung, all easily understood;

And thou hast no heart that can feel a delicate passion,
Nor canst thou know suffering after our weak human fashion.

Come tell why, from under thy quivering belly and filling
Thy curving *f*-holes, should come such melody thrilling.

Whence the song of the woods; the music of water falling;
The note of the love-lorn songster, mate to mate calling;

The laughter of children at play; the sigh of a maiden;
The breathing of zephyrs with perfume of evening laden;

The story of loves that are human; the joy of the angels;
The word of great peace, as if sung by mercy's evangels?

Come tell why, from under thy quivering belly and welling
From curving *f*-holes, should come that melody telling

Of sadness, and gladness, of pain, and anger, and sorrow,
Of doubt for today, and darker despair for tomorrow;

The crying of pris'ners; the moan and the groan of lost
          souls;
And sounds that might come from the banqueting table of
          ghouls.

The heart of a pine, didst thou grow on some green
          mountain side,
And didst fix in thy fiber all the melodious tide

Of the anthems of nature that float through the wood,
That magnificent temple, first house of our God?

Didst thou hear the birds sing in the sunshine fair,
And the roar of the lion rushing forth from his lair?

Did the thunder roll o'er thee its note of deep bass,
And the storm catch and sway thee in rugged embrace?

Did the wild mountain stream, all limpid and clear,
Go dancing beneath thee, thy rootlets to cheer?

And, thus, the whole octave of nature's glad scale,
As well as her minor note's saddening wail,

Become part of thy being, the soul of thy soul?
Did thy fiber, entrapping, imprison the whole?

'Neath the blow of the axe did thy trunk sway and fall?
Did they build thee in castle, or low cottage wall,

And, there, with the passage of joy laden years,
And days that were burdened with dropping of tears,

Didst thou hear every note of the human voice
Wherewith mortals lament and mortals rejoice?

The dirge and the cradle song, the gay wedding march—
Didst thou listen to all from some window arch?

The song of the chase; and the bugle's shrill call,
When warriors assembled—didst thou hear it all,

And, now, is thy soul with such music replete
That, to us, thou art able each note to repeat?

Or, did Stradivari, when he marked thee out,
Gave bound to neck, to *f*-hole, and to bout;

With fingers deft arranged each part;
Tell thee the story of the human heart?

Did he compel thee, with some magic spell,
The story evermore, with art divine, to tell?

And needs it now alone to touch thy string
That story from thy inner soul to bring?

What? Speakest not? Thou wilt not tell thy riddle?
I've found thee out; I'll tell it all, old fiddle.

Mute thou must be, thou canst not speak or sing;
A single note of melody thou canst not bring,

Except when soulful fingers drip with pearly notes of joy,
Or, saddened by our human woes, thy trembling strings
          employ.

©

Little Buds.

The flowers are plucked by human hands
        To wither and decay;
        But little ones,
        To whom death comes,
        Borne far—Oh, far away,
Bloom fair, for aye, in heavenly lands.

Today, Tomorrow, Someday.

TODAY is a helper
  Who seldom will fail
Each task to make lighter;
  O'er all to prevail.

Tomorrow is thy friend?
  O then be thou taught
Not on him to depend:
  He may, and may not.

But Someday 's a truant,
  Whom no man has bound;
In promise, most fluent;
  In practice, not found.

Only to fill out a page
  Was I written and put in this place:
Men there are, in every age,
  Like me in greatest plenty,
Who serve no better purpose than to grace
Some wasted corner, otherwise, in space,
  And keep from being empty.

Day Dreaming.

A Dreamer of dreams, I built castles in air
Surpassingly wonderful, wondrously fair.

I finished and furnished as only in dream;
We garnish our fancies with beauties that seem.

I dreamed, in my dreaming, as others have done,
That fame was but waiting for me to be won.

I saw her near by, a most beautiful form,
And yielded my heart as if taken by storm.

I felt that none other my life e'er could bless.
And pressed, then, my suit with most eager address.

She seemed a coy maiden, but only required
My pictured ideals in matter attired.

She asked for the castle I built in the air,
As dower of her wifehood, to dwell with me there.

"Thou surely art mine, Maid," I eagerly said,
"When wooing 's so easy, we'll certainly wed."

I fell, then, to work with might and with main,
Builded stone upon stone, wall, turret and vane.

My castle complete, I turned 'round to my bride,
Besought her to come take her place by my side.

She curled her sweet lip, turned to leave me alone;
My castles in air were but hovels in stone.

I 'roused from my day-dream, content with my lot;
I could not build castles, but could build a cot.

I built, and I found me a dear little bride;
Then dreamed that fame saw us and, envious, sighed.

◎

*The Witness.

SIX ushers in full dress, standing three on a side,
  Two flower-girls, a page, and a maid,
 A blushing young bridegroom with a beautiful bride,
  And a clergyman sober and staid;

A best man to carry the ring in his pocket,
  With people and music and flowers;
We tie the knot fast and carefully lock it,
  Then subscribe ourselves
      Lovingly yours.

_____
*Written on a marriage certificate.

Tot's Prayer.

"MAMMA, Th'ressa 's bad—s'e scolded"—
Said my little Tot, who, folded

In my arms at evening gloaming,
Tired from romp and all-day roaming,

Nestled, sleepy eyes uplifting,
Even then to Nod-land drifting,—

"Tots so s'eepy—mamma tiss her—
Put her down'—will mamma miss her,

When 'e 'ittle p'ayers all said
Mamma's Tot is put away in bed?"

Then she knelt with ringlet's dropping
Over shoulders white and sloping,

Knelt, with little "tootsies" peeping
From the dress she wore when sleeping,

And, in accents sweet and thrilling,
All the room with incense filling,

Of a pure child's fervent praying,
Pressed her dimpled hands while saying

Her, 'Now I 'ay me down to s'eep,
I p'ay 'e 'ord my soul to keep;

If I s'ould die afore I 'ake,
I p'ay 'e 'ord my soul to take'—

Then began as I had taught her,
Precious, darling little daughter,

Never any friend forgetting,
Nor a single name omitting—

"Dod b'ess mamma,—an' my papa,
John,—an' Mawy,—Joe,—an' Ga'pa"—

There she paused, and as I listened,
Opened eyes where mischief glistened,

While she prattled on in praying,
Strangest things in child words saying,—

"But Dod 'emem'er, if 'oo p'ease,
When 'oo does tum to b'ess all 'ese,

'Mem'er, sure, Tot tells 'oo 'at again,
'At Theressa "isn't in it."   'Men."

Rosebud.

I

ONE day, when at last
    A winter had passed,
And the sun, from the lap of the storms,
    Was peeping at earth,
    And promising birth
Of the manifold beautiful forms
    Of Springtime;

    On the meadow edge,
    Just over a ledge
Of rocks, out of which gurgled a spring,
    There, where woodland trees
    Bend tops to the breeze,
And the birds come their matins to sing,
    In Summerland;

    'Twas there, in an angle
    Of fence-row, and tangle
Of rank briers and ferns, that I found
    A wild, little bush,

Beginning to push
Its way, silently, out of the ground,
    In springtime and Summerland.

II

"Thou art mine little bush;
I'll help thee to push
Out of darkness thy way into light;
    Thy buds shall be mine,
    Ev'n as they are thine;
Thou shalt never be out of my sight,
    In Summerland."

III

The Rosebush—my bride—
I sat by her side
On the edge of the meadowland green;
    We sang but one song,
    Through all the day long,
And none happier ever were seen
    In Summerland;

    We sang this one strain,
    Again and again,
While the sun shed upon us his beams:
    "Thou'rt mine, Rosebud sweet,

Our circle complete,
Let us spend the bright day as in dreams
Of springtime in Summerland.

IV

Into that bright land
There came a strange band,
Stealing silently over the lea;
Rosebud was taken
By angels to waken,
From our day dreams, my sweet bride and me,
In Summerland:

Now all the day long
We can sing no song,
And, at eventide, to us there floats,
On the rocky ledge,
At the meadow edge,
But the sound of the whip-poor-will's notes,
In the autumn of our Winterland.

▷··◁

Decoration Day.

BRING flowers; bring flowers;
    Bring flowers that are red,
    And strew them over the soldier's grave;
Heap high o'er the home of the dead;
Thick cover his low peaceful bed:
'Twas a crimson offering he gave.

Bring flowers; bring flowers;
Bring flowers that are white,
And strew them here, where the soldier lies;
Make snowy, make snowy and bright;
Deep cover with flakes pure and light:
Laud honor unsullied up to the skies.

Bring flowers; bring flowers;
Bring flowers that are blue,
And strew them over the grassy mound;
Thick bestrew with red, white and blue;
Fit colors to cover the true:
Let praise of heroes forever resound.

Finis.

THE tale of life will soon be told:
Both he who tells and he who hears,
Together, will lie outstretched, cold,
In death's embrace.   O let not tears
Be shed because our life is bended
So sharply toward the grave, but heed
Lest life, when rounded out and ended,
Too little incense of good deed
Can show, toward heaven ascended.

www.ingramcontent.com/pod-product-compliance
Lightning Source LLC
Chambersburg PA
CBHW021534270326
41930CB00008B/1239

* 9 7 8 3 7 4 4 7 9 9 3 6 2 *